NOTES

ON THE

EARLY LITERATURE OF CHEMISTRY.

BY

H. CARRINGTON BOLTON, PH.D.

VI.

PAPYRUS EBERS, THE EARLIEST MEDICAL WORK EXTANT.

[Reprinted from the American Chemist for November, 1875.]

PHILADELPHIA:
COLLINS, PRINTER, 705 JAYNE STREET.
1875.

NOTES ON THE EARLY LITERATURE OF CHEMISTRY.

VI.

PAPYRUS EBERS, THE EARLIEST MEDICAL WORK EXTANT.

In article IV. of these Notes* mention was made of the most ancient chemical manuscript extant, a Greek papyrus of Egyptian origin, preserved in the library of the University of Leyden, and supposed to date from the third century A. D. This manuscript has never been fully described, the little known of it is contained in *Kopp's Beiträge der Chemie*, vol. i. p. 97.

Quite recently the Astor Library,† New York, has come into the possession of a work far surpassing in antiquity the Leyden manuscript, and of infinitely greater interest and value to the student of the history of chemistry. This remarkable work is a fac-simile of an Egyptian medical treatise, written in the sixteenth century B. C., and consequently more than 3400 years old. Though strictly a medical work, it is of no less interest to the chemist than to the physician, and may therefore find appropriate mention in these Notes on the Early Literature of Chemistry.

G. F. Rodwell, F.R.S., author of "The Birth of Chemistry," in a recent letter to the Editor of the *Chemical News*, refers to our knowledge of Egyptian chemistry in the following language: "When we re-

* American Chemist, vol. iv. p. 288.

† The reading public is indebted to the liberality of the late Mr. William B. Astor for this rare and costly work, and the writer is under obligations to the librarian, Dr. E. R. Straznicky, for his courteous attention.

member that the science originated in Egypt, and that the very name is derived from an Egyptian source, we can but hope that, in the progress of Egyptian discovery, as valuable information in regard to the history of chemistry as has already been found in regard to astronomy, may be brought to light."

This Egyptian papyrus is a first and opportune response to the desire herein expressed. The title reads thus:—

"PAPYROS EBERS, *das Hermetische Buch über die Arzneimittel der alten Ægypter in Hieratischer Schrift.* Herausgegeben mit Inhaltsangabe und Einleitung versehen von Georg Ebers. Mit Hieroglyphysch Lateinischen Glossar von Ludwig Stern. Mit Unterstützung des Königlich Sächsischen Cultus Ministerium. Wilhelm Engelman. Leipzig, 1875. Zwei Bände, folio."

Translated, the title is as follows:—

PAPYRUS EBERS, the Hermetic Book of Medicine of the Ancient Egyptians, in Hieratic writing. Published, with Synopsis of Contents and Introduction, by George Ebers. With a Hieroglyphic-Latin Glossary by Ludwig Stern. Under the patronage of the Royal Bureau of Education in Saxony. Leipzig: William Engelman, 1875, 2 vols. folio.

The papyrus of which this work is a fac-simile reproduction, was discovered by the archæologist Ebers during his visit to Egypt in the winter of 1872–73. Ebers and his friend Stern were residing at Thebes, collecting archæological data, and there became acquainted with a well-to-do Arab from Luxor, who brought to them for sale a modern image of Osiris, and a papyrus of no special value. Suspecting that the Arab was holding in reserve objects of greater interest, Ebers offered him a considerable sum for any remarkable specimens in his possession. This induced the Arab to return on the following day, bringing with him a metallic case containing a papyrus roll enveloped in mummy cloths. Ebers immediately perceived he had a prize, but was unable to command the large sum of money demanded for it, until provided with the means through the liberality of a German gentleman, Max Günther, travelling in that vicinity.

According to the Arab's account, the papyrus had been discovered fourteen years previously by a man since dead. The original papyrus was discovered between the bones of a mummy in a tomb of the Theban Necropolis.

Ebers hastened back to Leipzig with his precious roll, and deposited it for safe keeping in the University Library of that city. And now, with the co-operation of an enterprising publisher, and the assistance of royal patronage, he places it at the disposal of the civilized world by reproducing it in these handsome volumes.

The papyrus, as received by Ebers, consisted of a single, solidly rolled sheet of yellow-brown papyrus of finest quality, 0·3 metre wide, and 20·23 metres long. It formed one enormous book, but was divided into 110 pages, which were carefully numbered. For purposes of preservation and exhibition in convenient form the roll has since been cut into several lengths.

The writing, which is exceedingly clear and regular, is partly in black and partly in red ink, the latter occurring at the heads of sections and in the expression of weights and measures. The characters are known as Hieratic, being a cursive form of the Hieroglyphic method of writing, and bearing the same relation to the latter that our ordinary written hand does to printed characters. Hieratic script resulted from attempts to simplify the forms and outlines of the ideographic characters employed in hieroglyphic writing, which is essentially a combination of picture writing with a phonetic system. Hieroglyphics, in ancient Egypt, was the written language of the people, and Hieratic writing was chiefly confined to the sacerdotal caste.

The papyrus Ebers is so marvellously well preserved that not a single letter is lacking in the entire roll. The material of the papyrus itself, the inner bark of *Cyperus Papyrus*, was examined by Prof. Schenck, Professor of Botany in the University of Leipzig, who established its identity with that of similar rolls, and pronounced it of remarkably good manufacture.

The age of the manuscript was determined by a consideration of three points :—

1. Palæographic investigations of the form of the written characters.

2. Occurrence of names of kings.

3. Examination of a calendar which occurs on the back of the first page.

These data enable Ebers to assign the writing to the middle of the sixteenth century, or, more precisely, 1552 B. C. Accepting this date—and it has been established beyond reasonable doubt—the writing was prior to the exodus of the Israelites ; in fact, according to the commonly received chronology, Moses, in 1552 B. C., was just 21 years of age.

The authorship of this ancient work is not revealed, but it bears internal evidence of being one of the six Hermetic Books on Medicine named by Clement of Alexandria (200 A. D.).

The Egyptian priests, who were also the physicians, in order to give greater authority to their writings, were wont to ascribe them to their gods, and their codified medical knowledge was generally ascribed to the god Thuti (or Thoth). In proof of this Ebers quotes the following passage from page 1, lines 8 and 9, of the papyrus in question : "Rā pities the sick ; his teacher is Thuti, who gives him speech, who makes this book, and gives the instruction to scholars, and to physicians in their succession."

This god Thuti, also written Thoth and Taaut, is the famous Hermes Trismegistus of the Greeks, the same who was regarded by the alchemists of the Middle Ages with superstitious reverence as the father of alchemy.

However this may be, all historians accord in representing Hermes as the inventor of arts and sciences. He first taught the Egyptians writing, invented arithmetic, geometry, astronomy, and music; gave laws to the people, and regulated their religious ceremonies.

At the time of Jamblichus, who lived A. D. 363, the priests of Egypt showed forty-two books, which they attributed to Hermes (Thuti). Of these, according to that author, thirty-six contained the history of all human knowledge; the last six of which treated of anatomy of disease, of affections of the eye, instruments of surgery, and medicines.

The papyrus Ebers is indisputably one of these ancient Hermetic works; a study of the synopsis of the contents, given further on, will justify this belief.

The recipes and prescriptions contained in this treatise are evidently collected from various sources, some of them being quoted from still more ancient writings. It bears internal evidence of having been used in the healing art, for the word "good" occurs in the margin in several places, written in a different handwriting from the body of the work, and with lighter colored ink.

Ebers thinks the compilation was made by the College of Priests at Thebes, basing his conjecture partly on the locality in which it was discovered. The other great Egyptian Universities were located at Memphis, Heliopolis, Sais, and Chennu.

Ebers gives a synopsis of the contents of the entire work, and a literal translation of the first two pages of the roll, reserving a commentary and fuller translation for a future publication. A hieroglyphic translation of a portion of the Hieratic manuscript also accompanies the plates; the latter, 107 in number, are faithful and beautiful reproductions of the original papyrus, in the same yellow-brown color. The second volume contains a Hieroglyphic-Latin Glossary by Stern. Before proceeding to give details of its contents, one more peculiarity is worth mentioning. Though the pages are carefully numbered, the figures 28 and 29 are omitted, while the text is continuous. Ebers conjectures that the writer either accidentally forgot his count, or abstained from using these numbers for superstitious reasons, the discussion of which we cannot here enter upon.

As already remarked, the work is divided into chapters or sections. We cannot give Ebers' synopsis in full, but a fair insight into the character of the treatise may be obtained from the selected headings of sections, and extracts here following :—

Contents of Papyrus Ebers.

Headings of chapters (selected).

The numbers refer to the pages of the papyrus.

1. Of the preparation of medicines.
25. Of salves for removing the *uhau.*
47. Catalogue of the various uses of the *Tequem* tree.
48. Medicines for curing the accumulation of urine and diseases of the abdomen.
55. The book of the Eyes.
65. Medicaments for preventing the hair turning gray, and for the treatment of the hair.*
66. Medicines for forcing the growth of hair.
79. Salves for strengthening the nerves, and medicines for healing the nerves.
85. Medicines for curing diseases of the tongue.
89. Medicines for the removal of lice and fleas.
91. Medicines for ears hard of hearing.
99. The Secret Book of the Physician. The science of the beating of the heart, and the science of the heart as taught by the priestly physician Nebsecht.

Ebers encountered immense difficulties in the work of deciphering this papyrus; as an example of the obstacles met, he gives the following literal translation of a diagnosis beginning on Plate XXXVI., line 4 :—

"Rules for the *re het*, that is, suffering in the pit of the stomach (pylorus or cardia). When thou findest anybody with a hardening of his *re het*, and when eating he feels a pressure in his bowels (*chet*), his stomach (*het*) is swollen, and he feels ill while walking, like one who is suffering from heat in the back, *tau nu peht*, then look at him when he is lying outstretched,†

* Verily, "there is no new thing under the sun" (Eccl. I. 9); hair invigorators, hair dyes, pain killers, and flea powders, were evidently fashionable 3400 years ago!

† It is curious to note here, that (according to Dunglison), Diodorus states, the priestly physicians of Egypt formed their diagnosis principally on the position which the patient assumed in bed.

and if thou findest his bowels hot and a hardening in his *re het*, then say to thyself, this is a liver complaint, *sepu pu n merest*. Then make thyself a remedy according to the secrets in botanical knowledge from the plant *pa chestet* and from scraps of dates. Mix it and put it in water. The patient may drink it on four mornings to purge his body. If after that thou findest both sides of his bowels (*chet*), namely, the right one hot, and the left one cool, then say of it: That is bile. Look at him again, and if you find his bowels entirely cold, then say to thyself: His liver (? *merest*) is cleansed and purified; he has taken the medicine, *sep nef sep*, the medicine has taken effect."

The following is the translation of the first four lines of Plate I.:—

"The Book begins with the Preparation of the Medicines for all portions of the body of a patient. I came from Heliopolis with the Great Ones from *Het aat* the Lords of Protection, the Masters of Eternity and Salvation. I came from Sais with the mother-goddesses who extended to me protection. The Lord of the Universe told me how to free the gods from all murderous diseases."

The work abounds in prescriptions, of which the following are samples :—

"Beginning of the Book of Medicines. *To remove illness from the stomach.*

"Rub up the seed of the Thehui plant with vinegar, and give the patient to drink.

"*The same for sick bowels.*

Caraway seed	. . . .	$\frac{1}{64}$ drachm.
Goose fat	. . . .	$\frac{1}{8}$ "
Milk	. . . . .	1 tenat.

Boil, stir, and eat.

"*The same:*

Pomegranate seed	. . .	$\frac{1}{8}$ drachm.
Sycamore fruit (?)	. . .	$\frac{1}{8}$ "
Beer	. . . . .	1 tenat.

Treat as above."

In the original, the arrangement of the substances and quantities in two columns is the same as here given. The weights are written in red ink.

Other prescriptions contain reference to pills made by mixing certain substances with honey and rolling them into little balls.

The weights and measures in this unique work, deserve a more lengthy notice than space will permit. A series of special signs indicate measures of volume, and figures with dots above them represent weights. The unit of weight employed is believed by Ebers to bear a close relation to the later Arabic Dirhem or Drachm, which is equivalent to about 48 English grains. But owing to the smallness of the quantities given in the recipes, the unit is probably double the drachm in value. This unit and its divisions are represented in hieroglyphics thus:—

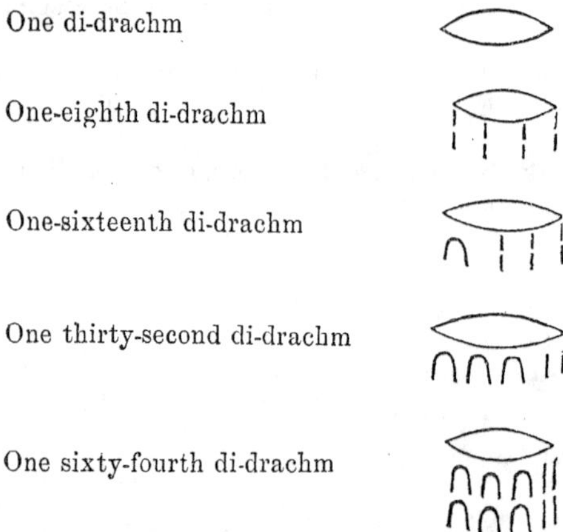

The fractions $\frac{1}{8}$, $\frac{1}{16}$, $\frac{1}{32}$, $\frac{1}{64}$ always recurring, and $\frac{1}{16}$ predominating, a quaternary arrangement which was superstitiously regarded as beneficial.

The unit of volume is thought to be the *tenat* which is equivalent to six-tenths of a litre. This unit and its subdivisions are represented by arbitrary signs of which the following is an attempt at reproduction.—

Unit or tenat.		
$\frac{1}{2}$	"	*or*
$\frac{1}{3}$	"	+
$\frac{1}{4}$	"	×
$\frac{1}{2}+\frac{1}{3}$ or $\frac{5}{6}$	"	
$\frac{1}{3}+\frac{1}{3}$ or $\frac{2}{3}$	"	+ +
$\frac{1}{3}+\frac{1}{4}$ or $\frac{7}{12}$	"	
$\frac{1}{4}+\frac{1}{2}$ or $\frac{3}{4}$	"	

When equal parts of the components of a prescription are taken, it is indicated by a light, short, vertical dash, placed opposite each substance thus |.

The writer failed to detect any sign at the beginning of the several recipes equivalent to the ℞ now used by physicians, and which, though generally regarded as the initial letter of the Latin word Recipe = take, has also been referred to an Egyptian source. This ℞ is said to have been originally the same as the symbol of Jupiter ♃, and to have been placed at the beginning of formulæ to propitiate the King of the Gods that the compound might act favorably.

The symbols in common use for scruples ℈, drachms ʒ, and ounces ℥, are said to have been derived from inscriptions on the ancient monuments of Egypt, and the resemblance of our sign for drachm to that of the $\frac{1}{2}$ *tenat* is certainly very striking.

Ebers states in his Preface, that notwithstanding there are to be found in this great work many incantations and conjurations, from which the priestly physicians could not abstain, still there is no hocuspocus nor gibberish in it, on the contrary, it shows that it was possible to write in the 16th Century B. C., complex recipes, and that they understood how to administer with care the medicines prescribed. Moreover, sorcery was forbidden in ancient times in the strongest manner, and the alchemistic Magi were punished in the reign of Rameses III. with death. The art of the physician was lost in the post-Christian era. Science became more and more tinged with magic, and was gradually obscured and degraded by it.

We cannot do better, in conclusion, than to quote the testimony of the learned Librarian of the Astor, with reference to the intrinsic value of this papyrus; he says:—

"It is hardly possible to exaggerate the literary, scientific, and historical importance of this remarkable document. It is the largest, best preserved, and most legible text in the language of Hieroglyphics, and does not speak vaguely of incomprehensible and fantastic ideas, but furnishes indubitable insight into different phases of the life of the ancient Egyptians."

School of Mines, Columbia College, N. Y.
November, 1875.

www.ingramcontent.com/pod-product-compliance
Lightning Source LLC
LaVergne TN
LVHW020641110826
845149LV00004B/1308

* 9 7 8 1 4 1 8 1 8 9 6 4 8 *